W9-ARZ-830

EXPLORING THE STATES
Georgia
THE PEACH STATE

by Lisa Owings

BLASTOFF! 5 READERS

BELLWETHER MEDIA · MINNEAPOLIS, MN

Note to Librarians, Teachers, and Parents:

Blastoff! Readers are carefully developed by literacy experts and combine standards-based content with developmentally appropriate text.

Level 1 provides the most support through repetition of high-frequency words, light text, predictable sentence patterns, and strong visual support.

Level 2 offers early readers a bit more challenge through varied simple sentences, increased text load, and less repetition of high-frequency words.

Level 3 advances early-fluent readers toward fluency through increased text and concept load, less reliance on visuals, longer sentences, and more literary language.

Level 4 builds reading stamina by providing more text per page, increased use of punctuation, greater variation in sentence patterns, and increasingly challenging vocabulary.

Level 5 encourages children to move from "learning to read" to "reading to learn" by providing even more text, varied writing styles, and less familiar topics.

Whichever book is right for your reader, Blastoff! Readers are the perfect books to build confidence and encourage a love of reading that will last a lifetime!

This edition first published in 2014 by Bellwether Media, Inc.

No part of this publication may be reproduced in whole or in part without written permission of the publisher. For information regarding permission, write to Bellwether Media, Inc., Attention: Permissions Department, 5357 Penn Avenue South, Minneapolis, MN 55419.

Library of Congress Cataloging-in-Publication Data

Owings, Lisa.
  Georgia / by Lisa Owings.
    pages cm. – (Blastoff! readers. Exploring the states)
  Includes bibliographical references and index.
  Summary: "Developed by literacy experts for students in grades three through seven, this book introduces young readers to the geography and culture of Georgia"–Provided by publisher.
  ISBN 978-1-62617-009-4 (hardcover : alk. paper)
  1. Georgia–Juvenile literature. I. Title.
  F286.3.O85 2014
  975.8–dc23
                                                                    2013002385

Printed in the United States of America, North Mankato, MN.

Table of Contents

Where Is Georgia?

Georgia stands in the southeastern corner of the United States. It is the largest state east of the Mississippi River. Alabama shares Georgia's western border. To the north are Tennessee and North Carolina. South Carolina runs along the northeastern border, and Florida lies to the south.

The Georgia coast meets the Atlantic Ocean in the southeast. Bays and the **mouths** of rivers break up the shoreline. Several small islands lie just off the coast. The state's capital and largest city is Atlanta. Its modern buildings rise over northwestern Georgia.

Alabama

N

W   E

S

Tennessee

North Carolina

South Carolina

Athens

★ Atlanta

Augusta

Georgia

Columbus

Savannah

Okefenokee
Swamp

Florida

Atlantic
Ocean

Gulf of Mexico

History

Native American hunters wandered into Georgia more than 10,000 years ago. Spanish explorer Hernando de Soto was the first European to arrive. He came in search of gold in 1540. English settlers followed in 1733. They founded the city of Savannah. The 1770s brought the **Revolutionary War**. American **colonists** won independence from Britain in 1783. Five years later, Georgia became the fourth state.

Hernando de Soto

Georgia Timeline!

1540: Hernando de Soto and his army arrive in Georgia.

1733: The first English colony settles in Savannah, Georgia.

1788: Georgia becomes the fourth state.

1793: Eli Whitney invents the cotton gin on a large cotton farm in Georgia. The machine helps southern farmers produce more cotton.

1838: The Cherokee people are forced to leave their homes. Thousands die as they travel to lands west of the Mississippi River. This journey is called the Trail of Tears.

1861-1865: Georgia and ten other southern states fight the northern United States in the American Civil War.

1929: Martin Luther King, Jr. is born in Atlanta, Georgia. He later leads the fight for equal rights for African Americans.

1976: Georgia native Jimmy Carter is elected the thirty-ninth President of the United States.

1996: Atlanta hosts the summer Olympic Games.

Eli Whitney

Martin Luther King, Jr.

Jimmy Carter

The Land

Georgia offers a wide variety of landscapes. The Appalachian Mountains stretch across the northern part of the state. Farther south, these forested mountains give way to gentle hills. The land flattens into **plains** in central Georgia. These **fertile** lands extend south and east to the Atlantic Ocean.

Many of the state's rivers flow into the Atlantic. These include the Altamaha and Savannah Rivers. The Flint and Chattahoochee Rivers flow south toward the **Gulf** of Mexico. The weather in Georgia is usually warm. Snow is rare. However, Georgians must watch out for storms. **Hurricanes** and tornadoes often sweep through the state.

Amicalola Falls

fun fact

Georgia's Amicalola Falls is the tallest waterfall in the southeastern United States. Its waters tumble 729 feet (222 meters)!

Did you know?

Providence Canyon in southwestern Georgia is called the "Little Grand Canyon." It was carved by water running off farmland.

Georgia's Climate

average °F

spring
Low: 51°
High: 75°

summer
Low: 69°
High: 90°

fall
Low: 54°
High: 76°

winter
Low: 36°
High: 58°

Appalachian Mountains

The Okefenokee Swamp

fun fact

Long ago, Native Americans walked on the floating islands of Okefenokee Swamp. They found that the land shook under their feet. They named the swamp the "land of the trembling earth."

Georgia is home to one of the largest swamps in North America. The Okefenokee Swamp lies on the state's southeastern border. It is green and full of life. In shallow areas, grasses poke through the water's surface. Bald cypress and giant tupelo trees reach into the sky. Their branches are draped in soft moss. In deeper areas, carpets of water lilies and floating hearts bloom. Islands of **peat** drift throughout the swamp.

alligator

Most of the Okefenokee Swamp is a wildlife **refuge**. More than 200 kinds of birds and over 40 different mammals make their homes there. The swamp is best known for the alligators that prowl its waters. Visitors can tour the swamp by boat or boardwalk.

Wildlife

Georgia's lands and waters are rich in wildlife. Black bears roam the northern mountains and southern swamps. Coyotes and bobcats hunt prey throughout the state. Wooded areas shelter deer and foxes. In swamps, beavers and otters keep watch for alligators. Herons and ibises grace the state's lakes and rivers.

Many **endangered** animals are at home off the coast. Right whales and humpback whales are sometimes spotted offshore. In shallow waters, gentle manatees feed on sea grasses. Several kinds of sea turtles **migrate** through Georgia waters. Some lay their eggs on island beaches.

coyotes

heron

manatee

black bear

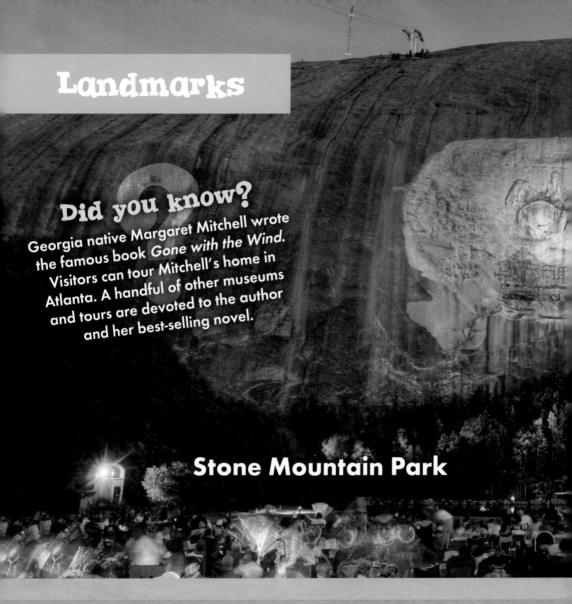

Landmarks

Did you know?
Georgia native Margaret Mitchell wrote the famous book *Gone with the Wind*. Visitors can tour Mitchell's home in Atlanta. A handful of other museums and tours are devoted to the author and her best-selling novel.

Stone Mountain Park

The city of Atlanta holds many attractions. The Georgia Aquarium is one of the largest in the world. Whale sharks, manta rays, and other sea creatures live in its more than 10 million gallons (38 million liters) of water. Nearby is the World of Coca-Cola. Visitors can learn about the soda's history and watch as it gets bottled.

Georgia Aquarium

Argentinosaurus

! **fun fact**

The Fernbank Museum of Natural History in Atlanta was the first to display a life-size model of *Argentinosaurus*, the world's largest known dinosaur.

Stone Mountain Park is one of the state's greatest landmarks. At its heart is a dome-shaped mountain. On one side of the mountain is a giant carving of three **Civil War** heroes. In Thomasville, Pebble Hill **Plantation** gives a sense of what life was like for wealthy Georgians in the 1900s.

Athens

Athens is a lively city in northeastern Georgia. It was founded in 1801 as the home of the University of Georgia. Since then, it has grown into one of Georgia's largest cities. Many of its original buildings survive. **Tourists** come to see the beautiful old mansions.

Athens is known as a center of culture and creativity. It is especially famous for its music scene. Rock bands R.E.M. and the B-52s got their starts there. The city's Morton Theatre once hosted jazz musicians Duke Ellington and Louis Armstrong. Big-name bands also flock to the stages of the 40 Watt Club and Georgia Theatre. Today, live concerts and music festivals draw fans of all ages to Athens.

Georgia Theatre

Working

Did you know?

Coca-Cola, Home Depot, Delta Air Lines, and UPS are all based in Georgia.

Long ago, most Georgians worked on farms. Today only a small number do. They tend crops of corn, cotton, peanuts, and pecans. Millions of peaches are also harvested each year. Many farmers raise chickens for their meat and eggs. Off the coast, fishers pull in nets full of shrimp, oysters, and clams.

Georgian soils are rich in clay. Its forests provide wood. Factory workers turn these materials into pottery and paper products. They also make packaged foods, clothing, and chemicals. Many Georgians have **service jobs**. They work in banks, airports, hotels, and restaurants. Some work in government buildings or on military bases.

Where People Work in Georgia

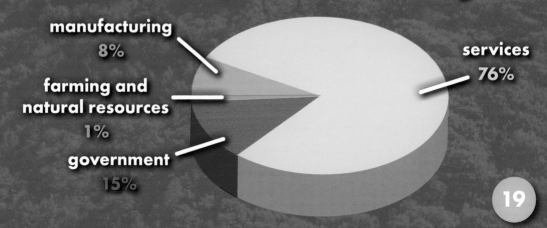

manufacturing
8%

farming and
natural resources
1%

government
15%

services
76%

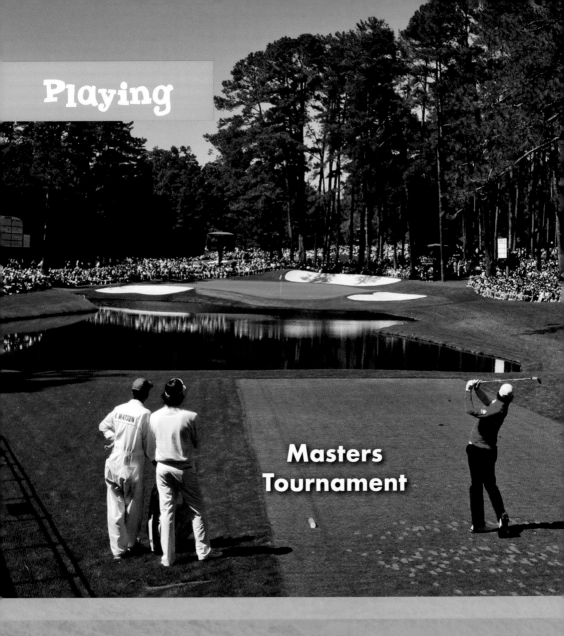

Playing

Masters Tournament

Sunny weather invites Georgians outdoors. The islands along the coast are popular vacation spots. Visitors can relax on sandy beaches or explore small towns and wildlife refuges. Adventurous Georgians hike, hunt, and fish in the many state parks.

fun fact

Georgia boasts the southern end of the Appalachian Trail. This hiking trail winds more than 2,000 miles (3,200 kilometers) through the mountains of the eastern United States.

Georgians in cities attend concerts or browse art and history museums. At home, many watch their favorite sports on TV. Football fans cheer on the Atlanta Falcons. Basketball fans root for the Hawks. Each April, Augusta hosts the world-famous Masters Tournament. Millions tune in to watch this golf event.

Peach Crisp

Ingredients:

4 cups sliced fresh peaches

1/3 cup white sugar

Topping:

1 cup rolled oats

1/2 cup packed brown sugar

2 tablespoons melted butter

1/2 teaspoon cinnamon

1 beaten egg

Directions:

1. Preheat oven to 375°F.

2. Toss the sliced peaches with the white sugar and place in a 2-quart baking dish.

3. Mix oats, brown sugar, butter, cinnamon, and salt together with a fork. Add the egg and mix until well combined.

4. Crumble mixture in small pieces evenly over the peaches. Bake for 35 minutes, or until the top is crisp and browned. Makes 6 servings.

Hint:

Best served warm and not right out of the oven. Serve with vanilla ice cream.

John Pemberton

Food in Georgia is influenced by many cultures. Native Americans grew corn in the state. They ground it up and mixed it with water. Today Georgians eat a similar dish called grits. Seafood is plentiful along the coast. Shrimp is often served over grits. Oyster stews and crab dishes are also popular.

Spanish explorers brought pigs to the area. Now barbecued pork is a celebrated dish. **Okra** and sweet potatoes give dishes an African flair. Another favorite is deep-fried chicken with collard greens and cornbread. A slice of peach or pecan pie is the perfect end to a Georgia meal.

Festivals

In spring, Georgians celebrate the flowers that bloom throughout the state. The Cherry Blossom Festival is held in Macon in March. Visitors enjoy a parade and free concerts as they admire the blooms. The Atlanta Dogwood Festival is held in April. Artists sell jewelry, pottery, and other fine art during this event.

The Savannah Music Festival is the largest music festival in the state. Spanning more than two weeks, it highlights music from classical to rock. The Pan-African Festival in Macon celebrates African and Caribbean cultures with music, storytelling, and food. Thousands come to Hiawassee each summer for the Georgia Mountain Fair. **Traditional** foods, **folk** music, and a **pioneer** village all showcase mountain life in northern Georgia.

Savannah's Saint Patrick's Day parade

fun fact

Saint Patrick's Day is a huge event in Savannah. The city hosts the second largest celebration in the country. A dazzling parade and other festivities attract up to a million visitors each year!

Georgians take pride in their traditional arts and crafts. During hard times, Georgians had to make many of their possessions with their own hands. These skills developed into art. Quilt making remains a popular craft. Georgians sew together pieces of fabric to make warm blankets. Some quilts have **geometric** designs. Others tell stories through pictures.

Georgia's clay-rich soils led to a tradition of pottery making. Jugs are often decorated with faces. Colorful glazes bring animal figures and other items to life. Basket weaving combines Native and African American traditions. Georgians weave beautiful containers from grasses, pine needles, and willow branches. The skill, creativity, and **diversity** of Georgia's people shine through these works of art.

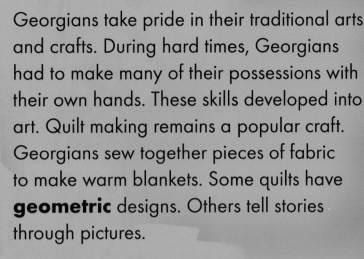

fun fact

Harriet Powers made some of the most interesting quilts in the South. The two that survive tell stories of the Bible and other historical events.

Fast Facts About Georgia

Georgia's Flag

Georgia's flag was adopted in 2003. It has three horizontal stripes of red and white. A blue square in the upper left corner has a circle of thirteen stars. They show that Georgia was one of the first thirteen states. In the center of the circle is Georgia's coat of arms.

State Flower
Cherokee rose

State Nicknames:	The Peach State The Empire State of the South
State Motto:	"Wisdom, Justice, Moderation"
Year of Statehood:	1788
Capital City:	Atlanta
Other Major Cities:	Augusta, Columbus, Savannah, Athens
Population:	9,687,653 (2010)
Area:	58,921 square miles (152,605 square kilometers); Georgia is the 24th largest state.
Major Industries:	services, manufacturing, farming, mining
Natural Resources:	clay, wood, farmland, marble, granite
State Government:	180 representatives; 56 senators
Federal Government:	14 representatives; 2 senators
Electoral Votes:	16

State Animal
right whale

State Bird
brown thrasher

Glossary

Civil War—a war between the northern (Union) and southern (Confederate) states that lasted from 1861 to 1865

colonists—people who settle new land for their home country

diversity—variety of cultures or backgrounds

endangered—at risk of becoming extinct

fertile—able to support growth

folk—relating to stories, customs, or practices that have been handed down from one generation to the next

geometric—using simple shapes and lines

gulf—part of an ocean or sea that extends into land

hurricanes—spinning rainstorms that start over warm ocean waters

migrate—to travel from one place to another, often with the seasons

mouths—places where rivers empty into larger bodies of water

native—originally from a specific place

okra—a green vegetable with a slippery texture

peat—plant matter that is found in wetlands

pioneer—relating to the first peoples to explore and settle an area

plains—large areas of flat land

plantation—a large farm that grows coffee, cotton, rubber, or other crops; plantations are mainly found in warm climates.

refuge—a protected area

Revolutionary War—the war between 1775 and 1783 in which the United States fought for independence from Great Britain

service jobs—jobs that perform tasks for people or businesses

tourists—people who travel to visit another place

traditional—relating to a custom, idea, or belief handed down from one generation to the next

To Learn More

AT THE LIBRARY

Benoit, Peter. *The Trail of Tears.* New York, N.Y.: Children's Press, 2012.

Cunningham, Kevin. *The Georgia Colony.* New York, N.Y.: Children's Press, 2011.

Garcia, Tracy J. *Eli Whitney.* New York, N.Y.: PowerKids Press, 2013.

ON THE WEB

Learning more about Georgia is as easy as 1, 2, 3.

1. Go to www.factsurfer.com.

2. Enter "Georgia" into the search box.

3. Click the "Surf" button and you will see a list of related Web sites.

With factsurfer.com, finding more information is just a click away.

Index

The images in this book are reproduced through the courtesy of: Natakuzmina, front cover (bottom); (Collection)/ Prints & Photographs Division/ Library of Congress, pp. 6, 7 (left), 7 (middle), 7 (right); Shuvabrata Deb, p. 8; SeanPavonePhoto, pp. 8-9, 16, 16-17, 28 (bottom); Randy Wells/ Getty Images, pp. 10-11; Juan Gracia, p. 11; Juan Martinez, p. 12 (left); JNB Photography, p. 12 (middle); Debbie Steinhausser, p. 12 (right); Glow Images, pp. 12-13; Christopher Meder, pp. 14-15; Newscom/ Reuters, p. 15 (bottom); Rob Wilson, p. 15 (top); Richard Green/ Alamy, p. 18; Val Thoermer, p. 19; MCT via Getty Images, pp. 20-21; Christine Glade, p. 21; Bon Appetit/ Alamy, p. 22; Msheldrake, p. 23 (top); Andre Jenny Stock Connection Worldwide/ Newscom, p. 23 (bottom); AP Photo/ Stephen Morton/ Associated Press, pp. 24-25; Marilyn Nieves, pp. 26-27; Rhonda Lee Willers/ African-American Artists/ Wikipedia, p. 27; Carsten Reisinger, p. 28 (top); Tom Hirtreiter, p. 29 (left); Brian J. Skerry/ Getty Images, p. 29 (right).